THE TRANSFORMATIVE POWER OF INCLUSIVE BUSINESS

CASE STUDIES ON HOW COMMERCIALLY VIABLE PROJECTS DRIVE DEVELOPMENT

Manfred Kiefer, Arvin Yana, and Christian Abeleda

DECEMBER 2024

ASIAN DEVELOPMENT BANK

ADB

6 ADB Avenue, Mandaluyong City, 1550 Metro Manila, Philippines
Tel +63 2 8632 4444; Fax +63 2 8636 2444
www.adb.org

ISBN 978-92-9277-077-8 (print); 978-92-9277-078-5 (PDF); 978-92-9277-079-2 (e-book)
Publication Stock No. SPR240580-2
DOI: http://dx.doi.org/10.22617/SPR240580-2

Note:
In this publication, "$" refers to United States dollars, "₱" refers to Philippine pesos, "₹" refers to Indian rupees, "MNT" refers to togrog, and "Rp" refers to rupiah.

On the cover: A day in the life of a Mongolian herder (photo by Bat-Erdene Batchuluun).

Cover design by Joseph Manglicmot.

CONTENTS

Driving development. An inclusive business project in Indonesia is transforming women from being mere consumers to becoming active contributors to the economy (photo by Robertus Pudyanto/ADB).

FOREWORD

The Asian Development Bank (ADB) is committed to promoting private sector-led growth. The impact of ADB-supported transactions varies based on the specific approaches and nature of the businesses involved, leading to a diverse range of beneficiaries. Projects that benefit low-income groups are particularly transformational, as these alleviate poverty, strengthen resilience, and reduce inequality. This publication, titled *The Transformative Power of Inclusive Business: Case Studies on How Commercially Viable Projects Drive Development*, explores innovative approaches that empower low-income communities.

As ADB deepens its focus on climate action, private sector development, regional cooperation, digital transformation, and resilience and empowerment, as outlined in its Strategy 2030 Midterm Review, promoting inclusive businesses is critical. This requires robust and close engagement with our private sector partners, who have played a catalytic role in accelerating progress on the sustainable development goals and advancing our transition to a net-zero future. Traditional business models focus on maximizing profits. Inclusive businesses, however, recognize their role as a force for social good, as engines for economic growth, and as partners for sustainability. Inclusive businesses also integrate low-income communities into value chains as producers, employees, or customers, unlocking new markets, driving economic opportunities, and fueling sustainable growth.

This publication delves into the transformative potential of inclusive business in our region as exemplified by the stories of five inclusive business projects. It showcases inspiring examples; explores key challenges and opportunities; and offers valuable insights for businesses, policymakers, and development practitioners alike.

ADB recognizes the significant role of the private sector in driving inclusive development. Through targeted investments, knowledge sharing, and capacity building programs, we are actively supporting the growth of inclusive businesses across Asia and the Pacific.

With total support of $3.05 billion for inclusive business projects from 2014 to 2023, ADB has significantly contributed to various inclusive business initiatives, accumulating a wealth of valuable lessons and experiences. This publication aims to document and disseminate these insights, allowing stakeholders to better understand the concept of inclusive business and its potential to empower disadvantaged populations. By underscoring effective models, lessons learned, and best practices, this publication seeks to offer replicable strategies that other projects, institutions, and geographical areas can adopt.

The Transformative Power of Inclusive Business: Case Studies on How Commercially Viable Projects Drive Development serves as a testament to our ongoing commitment to promoting innovative and sustainable solutions that empower people and communities. I encourage you to explore the wealth of information and perspectives within these pages as an inspiration to embrace the power of inclusive business for a more prosperous and inclusive future of our region.

Bhargav Dasgupta
Vice-President (Market Solutions)

ACKNOWLEDGMENTS

The authors would like to express their sincere gratitude to the following individuals for their invaluable support and assistance throughout the preparation and review of this publication:

To the management and staff of the Asian Development Bank's partner organizations for facilitating interviews with the beneficiaries featured in this publication, and for providing essential information that helped shape the project stories:

- Vicente Briones and Lailanie Moral of Center for Agriculture and Rural Development, Inc. (Philippines);
- Bharat Shah Joshi and Dinar Primasari of PT Cisarua Mountain Dairy Tbk (Indonesia);
- Madhvi Gupta and Ishika Rajveer of IIFL Home Finance Limited (India);
- Munkhnomin Bat-Erdene of Gobi Joint Stock Company (Mongolia); and
- Prateek Ghosal and Jasjit Singh of Ujala Cygnus Group of Hospitals (India).

To the Asian Development Bank Staff for their guidance, review, and validation of the contents of this publication, and for helping in country-level coordination:

- Carine Sophie Donges, Senior Investment Specialist, Private Sector Operations Department (PSOD);
- Doukas Doukidis, Senior Investment Specialist, PSOD;
- Pranav Mohan, Investment Specialist, PSOD;
- Tayyaba Rasheed, Investment Specialist, PSOD;
- Gevorg Sahakyan, Investment Specialist, PSOD;
- Matthew Young, Investment Specialist, PSOD;
- Yukitsugu Yanoma, Senior Natural Resources and Agriculture Specialist, Sectors Group;
- Neeti Katoch, Gender Specialist, Climate Change and Sustainable Development;
- Shannon Cowlin, Country Director, Mongolia Resident Mission;
- Mio Oka, Country Director, India Resident Mission;
- Pavit Ramachandran, Country Director, Philippines Country Office;
- Jiro Tominaga, Country Director, Indonesia Resident Mission;
- Rajesh Kumar Deol, Senior Communications Officer, India Resident Mission;
- Gantuya Ganzorig, Senior Communications Officer, Mongolia Resident Mission;
- Rosemarie F. Marquez, Senior Communications Officer, Philippines Country Office; and
- Andri Suryo, Senior Communications Officer, Indonesia Resident Mission.

ABBREVIATIONS

AB-PMJAY	Ayushman Bharat-Pradhan Mantri Jan Arogya Yojana
ADB	Asian Development Bank
BoP	base of the pyramid
CARD, Inc.	Center for Agriculture and Rural Development, Inc.
Cimory	PT Cisarua Mountain Dairy Tbk
COVID-19	coronavirus disease
EWS	economically weaker section
IIFL HFL	IIFL Home Finance Limited
LIG	low-income group
MSMEs	micro, small, and medium-sized enterprises
PMAY	Pradhan Mantri Awas Yojana
PSOD	Private Sector Operations Department
PPP	purchasing power parity
UCH	Ujala Cygnus Hospital

Cashmere for a brighter future. Mongolian herders engage in cashmere production to be able to provide their children with good education and improve their living standards (photo by Bat-Erdene Batchuluun/ADB).

Empowering women through affordable housing. Limited access to affordable housing hinders women's ability to achieve homeownership and financial independence (photo by ADB).

INTRODUCTION

Poverty remains a critical global issue, with an estimated 692 million people living in extreme poverty, defined as surviving on less than $2.15 per day (World Bank 2024).[1] Progress in reducing poverty in Asia and the Pacific was set back by at least 2 years because of the coronavirus disease (COVID-19) pandemic, and started to decrease again. However, a much larger segment of the low-income population deserves attention. Many of them are above the poverty line but live in vulnerable conditions, with some lacking access to basic goods and services; this can be addressed with market-based solutions.

Arranging a country's population based on per capita or per household income, starting from the lowest income groups at the bottom and ending with the highest income groups at the top, results in a pyramid-shaped graphic representation. The widest part of the pyramid represents the largest group (low-income individuals), while the narrowest part represents the smallest group (high-income individuals). The term "base of the pyramid" (BoP) refers to the population with the lowest income in a country.

---

1 Using 2017 purchasing power parity (PPP) prices, based on the World Bank data for 2024.

Depending on the concept[2] used, one-third to half of the world's population falls into the BoP category. Based on the World Bank thresholds for relative poverty, more than half (54.9%) of the 4.7 billion people in Asia and the Pacific live at the BoP, while 5.7% live in extreme poverty. Often, these groups are poorly served, are part of the informal economy, or live in rural areas. These people are often seen as relatively unattractive commercially and uncompetitive. Their consumption pattern skews toward food and, as incomes rise, a huge share goes toward housing, followed by transport, telecommunication, and health. All the while, they still struggle to cover their basic needs.

This group collectively creates significant demand for goods and services, yet these markets are still underserved. Business opportunities are missed because of a lack of information and experience with effective strategies.

The repercussions of inequality and poverty extend well beyond mere financial loss. They impact social frameworks, health conditions, psychological well-being, education, and social mobility. Furthermore, certain demographics—notably women, rural populations, and marginalized communities—are disproportionately represented. Economic disparities hinder access to quality education and limit opportunities for upward mobility. Poor living conditions often result in inadequate housing and lack of access to clean water and sanitation, exacerbating health problems. Additionally, social exclusion and lack of participation in economic and civic life further entrench poverty. Creating opportunities to lift individuals out of poverty and stabilize household incomes is essential for improving personal welfare and attaining wider societal objectives, including diminishing conflict and supporting sustainable development.

The private sector, with its unique capabilities, has the potential to significantly impact poverty alleviation efforts. Through its ability to create employment, drive economic growth, and foster innovation, the private sector can play a pivotal role in addressing this global issue. By leveraging its resources, expertise, and agility, the private sector can also complement the public sector's initiatives and programs, contributing in diverse ways to the complex challenge of poverty.

Inclusive business is one way in which the private sector contributes to promoting sustainable development and economic growth, and reducing inequality and poverty. Commercially sustainable private enterprises that integrate low-income segments into the mainstream economy as consumers, suppliers, distributors, and employees not only aim to generate reasonable economic returns but also create tangible development impacts by providing better income opportunities, jobs, and suitable goods and services to low-income groups.

2 UBS estimates this group at 2.8 billion people based on an income threshold of $10,000 per year (UBS 2023). When using the PPP concept, which is more suitable for developing countries, and the thresholds of the World Bank for relative poverty ($2.15 for Low-Income Countries, $3.65 for Lower Middle Income Countries, and $6.85 for Upper Middle Income Countries, all in 2017-PPP) 3.6 billion people belong in the BoP. Hammond et al. (2007) counted in their publication, that draws attention to this group, 4 billion based on a threshold of $3,000 (2002-PPP).

Inclusive business models often use specific impact mechanisms to achieve their objectives (ADB 2018) and can be categorized by their engagement channel:

The **consumer-focused model** targets underserved or low-income consumers by offering products or services tailored to their needs and affordability. Its impact mechanisms include improving the lives of consumers by providing access to essential goods and services, financial inclusion, quality education, or health care.

The **supplier-focused model** focuses on creating economic opportunities for marginalized or disadvantaged groups by integrating them into commercial supply chains. Its impact mechanisms include small-scale farmers, homestay providers, or producers of handicrafts or other products, and the model often capitalizes on their entrepreneurial skills. By sourcing goods or services from these groups, businesses can contribute to income generation and skills development.

The **employee- or distributor-focused model** involves hiring or empowering people from low-income groups. The approach often includes providing vocational training and skills development while targeting employees or sales agents with disadvantaged backgrounds. The impact channels may involve recruiting them to distribute products or services in underserved markets, expanding market reach, and incorporating financial services into the distribution network. These initiatives frequently have low-income populations as end consumers, which then turns the socioeconomic background of the sales agent or employee into a significant advantage.

Creating opportunities for women. The Miss Cimory program in Indonesia is an example of an employee- or distributor-focused model of inclusive business, which aims to create value for low-income or marginalized women by providing them with income-generating opportunities, skills development, and access to markets (photo by Robertus Pudyanto/ADB).

This publication features five inclusive business projects with innovative and replicable practices, organized by their integration modalities.

CONSUMER-FOCUSED MODEL

1. **Philippines: CARD Promoting Access to Finance for Low-Income Microborrowers Project.** This project focuses on providing financial services to low-income microborrowers, enhancing their access to credit and promoting economic inclusion.

2. **India: IIFL HFL Supporting Access to Affordable Green Housing for Women Project.** This project aims to offer affordable, sustainable housing solutions to women, integrating them into the housing market as consumers and promoting gender equality.

3. **India: Cygnus Affordable Hospitals Project.** The project provides quality health-care services to low-income populations in India, ensuring that essential medical care is accessible and affordable.

PRODUCER-FOCUSED MODEL

4. **Mongolia: Gobi Climate-Resilient Cashmere Value Chain Project.** This project supports low-income cashmere suppliers and integrates them into a sustainable value chain.

EMPLOYEE- OR DISTRIBUTOR-FOCUSED MODEL

5. **Indonesia: Cimory Inclusive Dairy Value Chain Project.** This project involves low-income women as distributors in the country's dairy industry.

Through these case studies, this publication illustrates how inclusive business initiatives can effectively integrate low-income segments into commercial markets, thereby driving inclusive economic growth and development.

Building a sustainable future for cashmere herders. An ADB project supports low-income cashmere suppliers in Mongolia and integrates them into a sustainable value chain (photo by Bat-Erdene Batchuluun/ADB).

INCLUSIVE BUSINESS—OVERVIEW AND KEY CONCEPTS

The phrase "inclusive business" was coined in the early 2000s and received global acknowledgment in 2015 when the G20 worked on a concept of inclusive business (International Business Action Network 2021). According to the G20's definition, "inclusive businesses provide goods, services, and livelihoods on a commercially viable basis, either at scale or scalable, to people living at the BoP, making them part of the value chain of companies' core business as suppliers, distributors, retailers, or customers."

ADB categorizes a business entity as supporting inclusive business if it achieves significant development impact by enhancing access to goods and services for the BoP population and/or offering income and/or employment opportunities to low-income individuals as producers, suppliers, distributors, employers, and/or employees (ADB 2018). ADB also specifies that an inclusive business must be commercially viable (i.e., its business model must be sustainable without subsidies) and can operate as an independent business entity or as part of a larger business entity. Unlike traditional corporate social responsibility initiatives, inclusive business aligns core business objectives with social goals, creating mutual benefits for companies and communities.

The BoP includes a diverse range of individuals and refers to those who are financially constrained and lack access to goods, services, and opportunities. It comprises not only extremely poor people but also those at risk of falling back into poverty.

IMPORTANCE OF INCLUSIVE BUSINESS

Inclusive businesses play a vital role in driving sustainable economic growth and fostering social development. These practices have a transformative impact by effectively integrating marginalized populations into business value chains, thus creating opportunities for empowerment and economic inclusion.

From a company perspective, inclusive business models may offer unique benefits if they enable companies to reach large, underserved markets. Companies that embrace inclusive business have the capacity to design compelling products and services targeted toward low-income populations.

For investors, inclusive businesses offer new markets and the potential for financial returns and sustainable investment opportunities while also giving them a net positive social impact. This dual benefit aligns financial and social goals, making inclusive businesses a compelling investment choice.

Governments need to understand inclusive business concepts to enable frameworks that engage the private sector in addressing social issues like poverty. By implementing specific policies, governments can create an environment conducive to inclusive business adoption, inclusive growth, and the creation of more and better job opportunities.

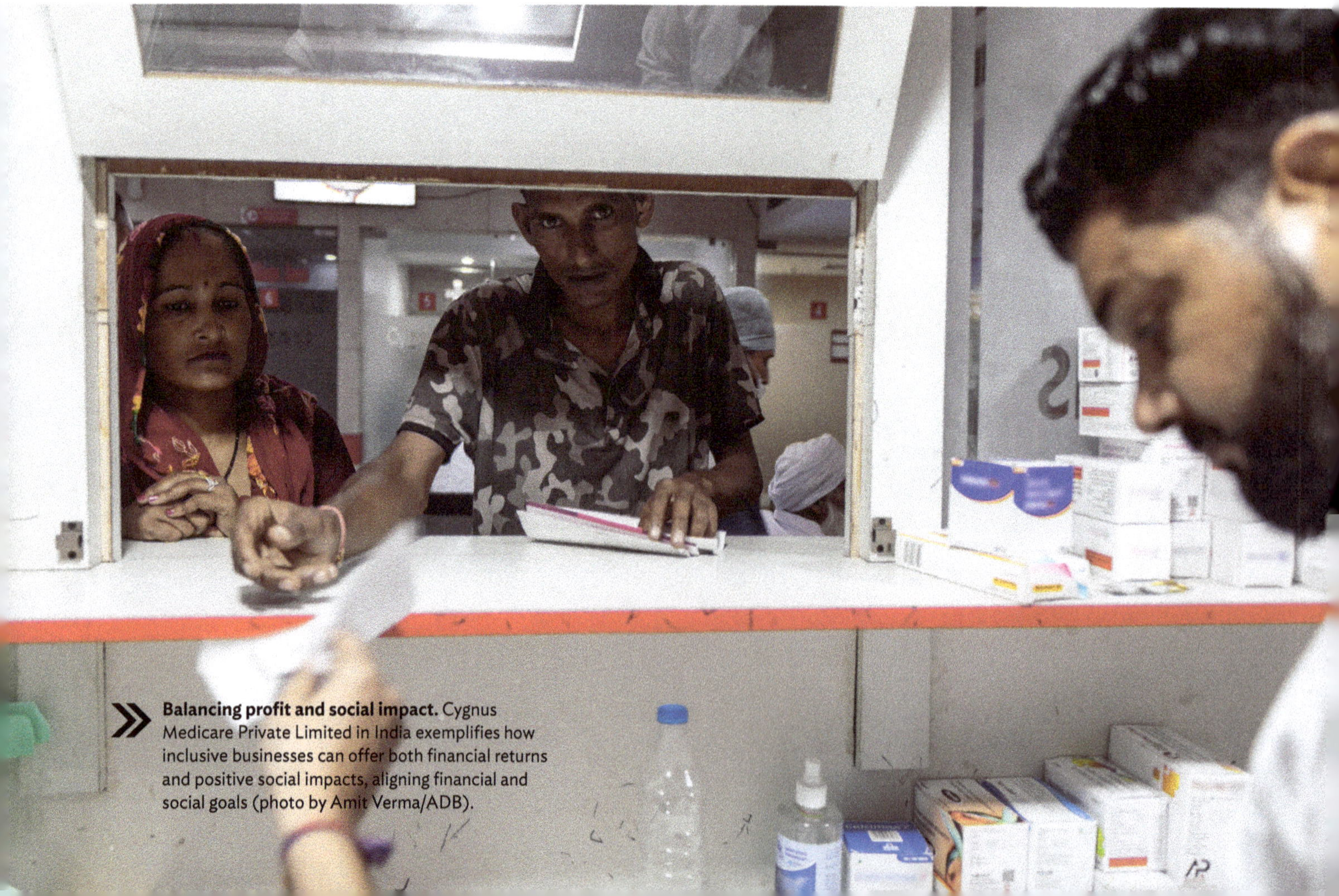

Balancing profit and social impact. Cygnus Medicare Private Limited in India exemplifies how inclusive businesses can offer both financial returns and positive social impacts, aligning financial and social goals (photo by Amit Verma/ADB).

FEATURES OF INCLUSIVE BUSINESS

The International Business Action Network (2021) described four distinct features of inclusive business. First, an inclusive business intentionally engages with the BoP. The Asian Development Bank (ADB) considers those who are aware of the benefit to the BoP as inclusive businesses. This involvement of the BoP in various business activities, such as supplying, distributing, retailing, working, or being customers, is not just a business strategy but a way to create positive social changes. These changes include better job opportunities, better livelihood, and improved access to affordable goods and services for the BoP. Whether driven by a business opportunity, a desire for social impact, or both, the positive impact on low-income populations is a direct and intentional outcome, not just a side effect. Additionally, it is about treating people at the BoP as partners and customers rather than just beneficiaries.

Second, inclusive businesses need to be financially viable to ensure that the business and its effects are long-lasting and support itself. Having a business plan that works for the long term should ensure continuity.

Third, the inclusive business scaling potential is crucial. This potential allows the inclusive business to expand its operations or customer base, thereby amplifying its social impact. It is not just about growing for the sake of growth but also about meeting the demand for relevant products and services based on the company's operational model. This scaling potential is a testament to the adaptability and relevance of inclusive businesses in addressing the needs of the BoP.

Lastly, it is crucial to measure and manage impact to achieve positive outcomes for the BoP. Through this, inclusive business companies can gain a comprehensive understanding of their impacts and adapt their processes and business models flexibly to the needs of the BoP.

Inclusive business represents a transformative approach to achieving sustainable development by aligning business success with social progress. By adopting inclusive business models and strategies, companies can unlock new markets, drive innovation, and reduce poverty and inequality.

Supporting sustainable cashmere. An ADB loan is supporting the sustainable procurement of raw cashmere from Mongolia's local herders while also contributing to climate-resilient practices (photo by Bat-Erdene Batchuluun/ADB).

INCLUSIVE BUSINESS
CASE STUDIES

Supporting women micro-entrepreneurs. A microloan from the Center for Agriculture and Rural Development, Inc. allows Rowena Sedeño (seated, left) to successfully set up an e-loading and payment center business (photo by Al Benavente/ADB).

1

MICROFINANCE

EXPANDING FINANCIAL INCLUSION FOR LOW-INCOME WOMEN IN THE PHILIPPINES

PROJECT INFORMATION

Project Name	CARD Promoting Access to Finance for Low-Income Microborrowers Project
Company	Center for Agriculture and Rural Development (CARD), Inc. (A Microfinance NGO)
Country	Philippines
ADB loan	$10 million
Approval Date	3 August 2021
Development Goal	Increase access to finance for low-income women and microborrowers in the Philippines

In Quezon City, the most populous city in the Philippines, Josefina Maranan and Rowena Sedeño share a common journey of resilience and empowerment as women micro-entrepreneurs. Both are supported by the Center for Agriculture and Rural Development Inc. (CARD, Inc.)—a microfinance nongovernment organization dedicated to poverty alleviation and rural development through commercially driven microfinance and community development programs—to pursue their entrepreneurial dreams and achieve their families' aspirations.

COMPANY PROFILE

Center for Agriculture and Rural Development, Inc.

CARD, Inc. is a nongovernment organization in the Philippines that provides microloans and microinsurance, in partnership with registered microinsurance providers, to empower socially and economically challenged women and families. With 2.96 million clients served so far, primarily women, and a repayment rate of 99.38%, CARD, Inc. operates on a cost-covering business model without relying on grants or subsidies. Founded by Jaime Aristotle Alip, referred to by some as the "father of microfinance in the Philippines," the organization is part of CARD Mutually Reinforcing Institutions (CARD MRI), which includes 29 other companies supporting a poverty reduction mission.

Year Founded	1986
Head Office	Laguna Province, Philippines
Primary Industry	Microfinance
No. of Employees	7,606
Number of Active Clients with Loans	1.912 million
Number of Office Units	3,123
Loans Outstanding	₱16.14 billion ($277 million)
Total Asset	₱25.59 billion ($439 million)
Website	www.cardmri.com/cardinc

Maranan, a housewife, sought to supplement her family's income by starting a small aquatic pet shop. Determined, and with the assistance of CARD, Inc., she expanded her inventory in 2023 through a ₱20,000 ($350) loan, stocking up on fish, fish food, and other aquatic supplies. This allowed her to meet growing demand as businesses recovered from the pandemic. This loan was payable at ₱515 ($8.73) weekly over a year.

Similarly, Rowena Sedeño found her entrepreneurial success through CARD, Inc. After trying various businesses, including a grocery store and a restaurant, she finally found her niche with an e-loading and payment center business that was boosted in 2023 through a ₱100,000 ($1,748) loan, her latest and largest from CARD, Inc., payable at ₱2,560 ($44.70) per week over a year. The loan provides the necessary working capital to handle large outgoing remittances and fund her business operations.

Powering potential. Micro-entrepreneurs need access to finance to be able to take advantage of and maximize the opportunities they spot in their local communities (photo by Al Benavente/ADB).

Driving the Philippine economy. Micro, small, and medium-sized enterprises, including the e-loading and payment center business of Rowena Sedeño, form the backbone of the Philippine economy, comprising 99.6% of all businesses (photo by Al Benavente/ADB).

Maranan's and Sedeño's enterprises are among the micro, small, and medium-sized enterprises (MSMEs) that serve as the backbone of the Philippine economy, accounting for 99.6% of all business establishments and 65.1% of the country's workforce in 2022 (Philippine Department of Trade and Industry n.d.). MSMEs contributed about 40% of gross domestic product in 2020 (UNDP 2020). More than half of MSMEs operate in wholesale and retail trading, and food manufacturing.

Most MSMEs are small, with annual gross revenues below ₱1 million ($20,000), and more than 70% are led or founded by women (Asia Pacific Foundation of Canada 2018). These localized businesses predominantly employ workers from nearby locations and of similar socioeconomic backgrounds. Typically, employees of MSMEs are generally poor and have low educational attainment. This highlights the role MSMEs play in providing livelihoods to marginalized communities.

"A significant portion of the Philippine population, being a developing country, grapples with widespread poverty and faces limited access to financing opportunities," said Vicente Briones, Jr., executive director of CARD, Inc.

Despite their economic significance, MSMEs in the Philippines face substantial challenges, primarily because of limited access to capital. Access to funding is often essential for micro-entrepreneurs to take advantage of the opportunities they identify within their local environment.

Business owner Rowena Sedeño counts the day's sales after closing (photo by Al Benavente/ADB).

However, local banks tend to perceive MSMEs as high-risk borrowers because they lack credit history and have limited management and financial capabilities. Serving them comes with high administrative costs because of the small amounts MSMEs need or are able to borrow (Khor, Sebastian, and Aldaba 2013). This risk perception makes it difficult for MSMEs to secure the necessary financing to sustain and grow their businesses.

The COVID-19 pandemic exacerbated these challenges, severely impacting microborrowers, who were among the hardest-hit segments of the Philippine economy. Extended lockdowns and ongoing uncertainty forced many microborrowers to close their businesses as revenues plummeted. The pandemic also disrupted household incomes because of job losses and salary cuts. Restrictions on cross-border travel hindered the deployment of migrant labor, aggravating joblessness and reducing remittances (UNICEF 2020).

As COVID-19 created a greater need for borrowing capacity and capital, CARD, Inc. saw an opportunity to collaborate with ADB to expand financial inclusion in the country, driven by a shared vision for empowering people and communities. CARD, Inc.'s capacity to provide livelihoods to microborrowers, mostly low-income women and farmers, was further enhanced with ADB's $10 million loan package. The loan enables CARD, Inc. to reach more microborrowers, particularly in remote and underserved areas, providing essential financial resources to those who typically lack access to conventional banking services. By supporting those affected by the economic disruptions of COVID-19, the project helps in the recovery and sustainability of small businesses, thereby stabilizing household incomes and enhancing community resilience.

ACCELERATING MICROBUSINESS OPERATIONS

Maranan's journey with CARD, Inc. began in 2010 with a first microloan of ₱3,000 ($53). After the pandemic, it was also CARD, Inc. that brought her business back to life. CARD, Inc. helped Maranan recover from the pandemic when her pet shop temporarily closed down because of COVID-19 restrictions.

"As a plain housewife, I am amazed that a company would trust me to borrow money. It's empowering," Maranan shared, adding that she had always dreamed of contributing to her family's income despite her husband's steady, albeit low-paying, job as a private school teacher. Her positive experience led her to encourage her family members to join CARD, Inc. as well.

"As a family, our goal was to send our children to school and have food on the table. CARD, Inc. helped us achieve this with their education loans and microloans," Maranan recalled.

Other financing institutions, she said, had higher interest rates, but CARD, Inc.'s rates appeared to be much lower. "They lend money with a heart, offering reasonable interest and terms," she said.

Maranan appreciated the straightforward loan application process, which required only a business proposal, site verification by an account officer, and validation by the unit manager.

Sharing success. Pet shop owner Josefina Maranan shares her experience with the Center for Agriculture and Rural Development, Inc.'s new customers (photo by Al Benavente/ADB).

"My determination to succeed was my only collateral, and it motivates me to make timely payments and build a good credit history," said Maranan.

Since obtaining the loan in 2023, her pet shop's earnings have doubled, providing financial stability for her household.

Sedeño has been a client of CARD, Inc. since 2007, and her latest loan helped her expand her e-loading and remittance business services. CARD, Inc. uses membership as a tool to build trust, provide financial education, and gradually increase credit limits.

"CARD, Inc. was always part of our financial journey, from the time we were still experimenting until we found a good business," Sedeño said.

Her business flourished as the only payment center in a village of 1,000 households. With the profits, Sedeño built two houses for her family of six and purchased a car. She also benefited from CARD Inc.'s training programs, such as on bookkeeping.

CARD, Inc.'s philosophy encourages clients to develop alternate income streams, ensuring a safety net in case one's primary income source is disrupted. This led Sedeño to work at the same time as an online tutor and a real estate agent. "Because of CARD, Inc.'s help, we have obtained financial freedom. Now, we can buy not just our needs but also our wants," she said.

Determined to succeed. Josefina Maranan applied for a microloan from the Center for Agriculture and Rural Development, Inc. with her determination to succeed as her only "collateral" (photo by Al Benavente/ADB).

Serving the underserved. The Center for Agriculture and Rural Development, Inc. offers financial services to low-income individuals without requiring collateral, focusing on underserved areas (photo by Al Benavente/ADB).

Through their entrepreneurial efforts and the backing of a supportive lender, these two women have transformed their families' lives, embodying resilience, financial stability, and empowerment.

INCLUSIVE BUSINESS STRATEGY

CARD, Inc.'s inclusive business model is designed specifically to cater to the needs of low-income individuals and communities. By focusing on this market segment, they are better able to understand the unique challenges and opportunities present in serving clients with limited resources. CARD, Inc. utilizes an individual lending methodology, where borrowers apply individually through small groups, called centers. In this approach, borrowers' family members act as co-borrowers who share the obligation to repay the loan. This approach not only helps mitigate the risk of default but also fosters a sense of responsibility among family members, which can improve loan repayment rates.

Unlike traditional banks, CARD, Inc. does not require collateral from its borrowers because the organization's primary mission is to provide financial services to low-income individuals (often in underserved or impoverished areas) who do not have assets or property suitable as collateral. It also helps borrowers build savings and capital by requiring regular deposits, in accordance with government policies for nongovernment organizations. Borrowers must deposit at least ₱50 ($0.86) weekly, which the borrowers can withdraw after availing themselves of a loan. CARD, Inc. offers a higher interest rate on these deposits than commercial banks to encourage saving.

CARD, Inc. reaches out to potential clients nationwide. Low-income clients are recruited in two ways. In areas with an existing office, CARD, Inc. relies on referrals from clients. In areas with no existing offices, account officers coordinate with mayors and *barangay* (village) officials to identify poor families and potential clients. If there are at least 20 potential clients, CARD, Inc. sets up a center in the area.

CARD, Inc. uses the Poverty Probability Index[3] tool to screen potential microfinance clients and measure poverty. "Through this tool, we do not only have the full understanding of the economic status and poverty levels of our potential clients, but we are able to tailor our loan products, repayment schedules, and support services to suit the needs and capabilities of borrowers better," said Vicente Briones, Jr., CARD, Inc.'s executive director.

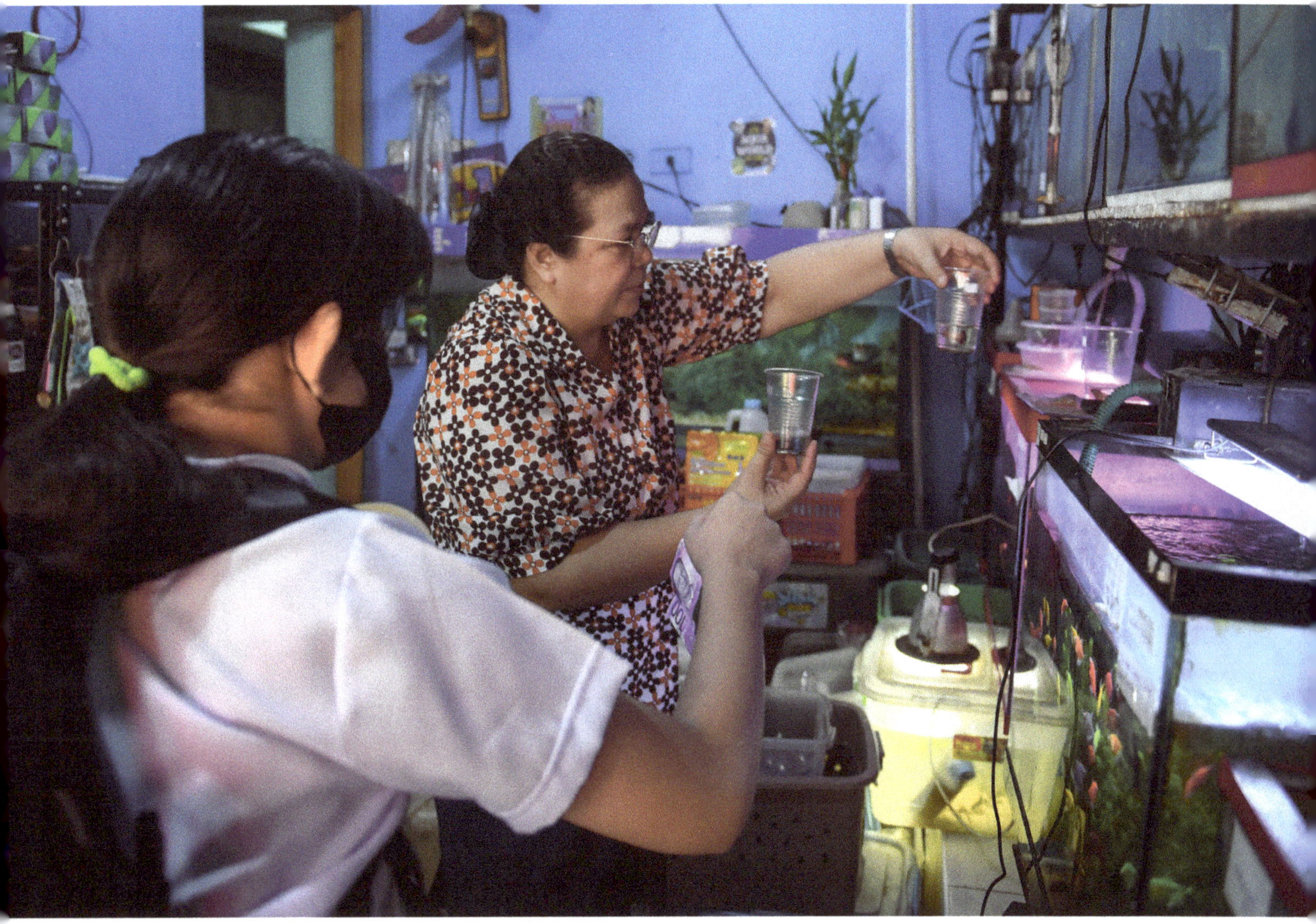

Maranan attends to a customer of her aquatic pet shop (photo by Al Benavente/ADB).

[3] The Poverty Probability Index is a tool used by organizations, particularly in the microfinance and development sectors, to measure the likelihood that a household is living below the poverty line.

> **Through the Poverty Probability Index tool, we do not only have the full understanding of the economic status and poverty levels of our potential clients, but we are able to tailor our loan products, repayment schedules, and support services to suit the needs and capabilities of borrowers better.**
>
> Vicente Briones
> Executive Director
> Center for Agriculture and Rural Development, Inc.
> Philippines

Unlike other microfinance institutions, CARD, Inc. integrates a comprehensive range of services into its microfinance model, including insurance, credit, savings, education, and health services. This holistic approach supports the financial and nonfinancial needs of its clients, aligning with CARD, Inc.'s vision to establish a client-owned bank.

Briones said this vision emphasizes not only access to financial services but also ownership and control, with clients actively participating in decision-making processes. CARD, Inc. prioritizes women who demonstrate the capacity to repay loans and are in good physical health, empowering them through inclusive financial solutions and community involvement.

"CARD, Inc. recognizes that ADB's commitment to developing people and communities closely aligns with its own mission. This shared vision ensures that the partnership is rooted in common goals of promoting sustainable economic development and improving the lives of marginalized populations," Briones said.

With ADB funding, CARD, Inc. expanded its microfinance loans as of 31 December 2023 to 382,698 clients in 276 branches across the country, with total loans in 2023 amounting to ₱8.7 billion ($149 million).

Digital solutions for convenient banking. The Center for Agriculture and Rural Development, Inc. has embraced digital financial services to facilitate convenient and accessible transactions for their clients (photo by Al Benavente/ADB).

LESSONS AND KEY TAKEAWAYS

- Focusing on underserved and low-income individuals enables a deeper understanding of their unique challenges. Tailoring products and services to meet their specific needs is crucial for building trust and building long-term relationships.
- CARD, Inc.'s individual lending approach through small groups (centers), with family members acting as co-borrowers, strengthens borrower accountability and encourages repayment. This method mitigates risk by distributing responsibility across family units.
- Insisting on collateral would not work with low-income individuals who lack productive assets. A hands-on and inclusive approach can replace collateral as risk mitigation while simultaneously empowering borrowers and providing financial access to individuals typically excluded by traditional banking models.
- Requiring and incentivizing borrowers to make small, regular deposits builds financial discipline and encourages savings.
- Using tools like the Poverty Probability Index allows organizations to better understand the economic realities of their clients. This data-driven approach helps tailor loan products, repayment schedules, and support services to the specific needs of each borrower.

Unlocking women's potential. The Miss Cimory program is a social initiative designed to empower women by providing them with income opportunities as independent sales agents (photo by Robertus Pudyanto/ADB).

2

DAIRY AND CONSUMER FOOD PRODUCTS

SUPPORTING WOMEN AS SALES AGENTS IN INDONESIA'S DAIRY VALUE CHAIN

PROJECT INFORMATION	
Project Name	Inclusive Dairy Value Chain Project
Company	PT Cisarua Mountain Dairy Tbk (Cimory)
Country	Indonesia
ADB Financing	$4.2 million
Approval Date	27 October 2021
Financing Modality	Equity investment
Development Goal	Promote increased production of affordable nutritious dairy products to support the livelihoods of stakeholders across the dairy value chain

In the bustling streets of Padang Pasir, West Sumatra, 39-year-old Elmita Sari Dewi remembers navigating the challenges of earning a living as a street vendor, striving to support her family with meager daily earnings.

Her husband earned Rp2 million ($125) per month as a construction worker, which fell short of meeting the family's financial needs. Dewi recalls that when their three children had exams in their schools, they often had to send promissory letters because they could not pay their tuition fees on time.

From street vendor to Miss Cimory sales agent. Elmita Sari Dewi is back in the streets of Padang Pasir in Indonesia as a proud Miss Cimory sales agent (photo by Robertus Pudyanto/ADB).

However, her life took a transformative turn when she was recruited by the Miss Cimory distribution program, offering her an opportunity to become a sales agent for dairy products. What began as a leap of faith has blossomed into a remarkable journey of empowerment, economic independence, and community support.

“I used to struggle to make ends meet as a street vendor. At one point, I had to leave the streets because I ran out of capital. Joining Miss Cimory opened doors I never imagined. It provided me with the training, skills, and support I needed to succeed.”

The Miss Cimory distribution program is a social initiative of PT Cisarua Mountain Dairy Tbk (Cimory) that started in 2013, hiring exclusively female agents and training them to sell dairy products door-to-door. This selling approach allows agents to build personal relationships with customers, reach underserved markets, and educate customers about the benefits of Cimory products. The program provides an important avenue for women, especially low- to middle-income women with school-aged children who want to help their families participate in an empowering livelihood activity.

In 2021, ADB invested in Cimory to provide additional capital to expand its production and distribution capacities, including the Miss Cimory program. Cimory aimed to improve its market position and capitalize on growth opportunities in the dairy industry. Cimory is a renowned

COMPANY PROFILE

PT Cisarua Mountain Dairy Tbk

Cimory, officially known as PT Cisarua Mountain Dairy Tbk, is a well-known Indonesian company primarily engaged in the dairy and food processing industry. The family-owned Cimory has become a significant player in Indonesia's dairy sector. Cimory produces a wide variety of dairy products, including fresh milk, yogurt, and processed foods. The company is listed in Indonesia Stock Exchange (IDX: CMRY), and has been awarded as one of the Indonesia's best-managed companies. It aims to grow sustainably and become Indonesia's leading premium food and beverages manufacturer.

Year founded	2005
Head Office	Jakarta, Indonesia
Primary Industry	Dairy Products and Consumer Food
Number of Miss Cimory Agents	5,494
Number of Miss Cimory Centers	252 (as of 31 December 2023)
Net Sales	Rp7.77 trillion ($496 million)
Total Assets	Rp7.05 trillion ($449 million)
Website	www.cimory.com

Cultivating customer connections. Miss Cimory sales agent Elmita Sari Dewi delivers dairy products door-to-door, allowing her to build direct relationships with customers while expanding her sales network (photo by Robertus Pudyanto/ADB).

household dairy brand in Indonesia, which specializes in products like yogurts, flavored milk, processed meat, and egg-based products.

Miss Cimory deviates from traditional retail supply chains and operates with an exclusive female sales force. With operations spanning more than 30 cities across Bali, Java, and Sumatra islands, the program offers an opportunity for women to engage in safe and socially acceptable employment, often in areas with limited opportunities available to them.

INCLUSIVE BUSINESS STRATEGY

The Miss Cimory initiative enables Cimory to access markets often overlooked by conventional retail channels, especially in rural and semi-urban regions. By hiring local women as distributors through a direct sales method, Cimory can more effectively reach customers in these areas, boosting its market presence. Equipped with portable boxes and often familiar with the customers, Miss Cimory agents can easily navigate through neighborhoods to deliver their top products directly to customers' doorsteps. Cimory's growth contributes to providing new food choices, enhancing rural livelihoods, and empowering women economically, reflecting an inclusive business approach.

ADB's financing has created jobs for about 400 employees and expanded Cimory's sales agent network from 2,509 agents in 2020 to 7,000 by 2024, enabling more women to contribute to their households' income and have greater control over their finances and decisions.

Miss Cimory sales agents meet at their Padang Pasir office (photo by Robertus Pudyanto/ADB).

Miss Cimory agents broaden their customer base by reaching local communities in informal settings while promoting nutritious options for children (photo by Robertus Pudyanto/ADB).

Hendri Viarta, the current executive director of Cimory, shared how they designed the program to be inviting to women.

"The Miss Cimory program aims to empower women who may not have had access to higher education and are struggling economically. We strive to inspire them to dream big and equip them with the tools to turn those dreams into reality," Viarta said. "At the same time, the distribution model helps Cimory achieve cost-efficient market expansion by reducing the need for extensive infrastructure and lowering operational costs."

Farell Sutantio, Cimory's chief executive officer who co-founded the program with Viarta, said that "by encouraging women to achieve financial independence, and become leaders within their households and communities, we foster meaningful change."

"Investing in women generates a multiplier effect, benefiting not only businesses but also the entire nation," Sutantio said.

Cimory is using the ADB financing for expanding the Miss Cimory distribution network and for increasing its production capacity. This expansion will benefit an additional 4,200 dairy farmers. With more than 100,000 farmers, dairy is a significant industry in Indonesia. About 77% of domestic fresh milk comes from smallholder farmers who typically own just three cows each.

Women are vital in Indonesia's agriculture, contributing significantly to farming and milk production, yet their efforts are often overlooked. Despite performing many demanding and labor-intensive tasks, they usually lack decision-making power within households or communities (Kusumadewi and Soedjito 2018).

Indonesia is not free from gender biases and women have on average lower education levels; less business experience; and limited access to agricultural extension services, markets, and financial services. These factors prevent them from fully participating in household dairy businesses (Food and Agriculture Organization of the United Nations 2019). Traditional gender roles and norms often reinforce the idea that women should prioritize family and domestic duties over economic activities outside the home. This limits women's opportunities for economic empowerment in agriculture.

FROM STREET VENDOR TO SUCCESSFUL SALES AGENT

Dewi expresses gratitude for the training provided by Miss Cimory. "Learning about product knowledge and customer approach has been invaluable," she said. "It has not only

Empowering others. With her increased income as a Miss Cimory agent, Elmita Sari Dewi now has the financial means to support orphans, positively impacting their lives through her work (photo by Robertus Pudyanto/ADB).

Nurturing an extended family. Elmita Sari Dewi is joined by her immediate family, and the two kids she helps send to school (photo by Robertus Pudyanto/ADB).

boosted my sales but also enhanced my communication skills and visibility in the community."

Upon joining Cimory in 2022, she started earning Rp5.7 million ($356) per month. Through her dedication and hard work, she achieved her highest total monthly sales of Rp180 million ($11,249). Her current net income ranges from Rp10 million to Rp15 million ($633 to $950) per month, surpassing her husband's earnings. With her improved financial situation, she was able to purchase three motorcycles and a car. She said she no longer needs to write promissory notes to schools as they can now afford to pay their children's tuition fees. This has opened up brighter prospects for their children, with their eldest son planning to pursue a maritime degree after completing his senior high school education in 2024.

Dewi's efforts have not only boosted her family's income but also enabled her to give back to her community. She allocates a portion of her monthly earnings to support four orphans, ensuring they receive the education they need.

This inclusive business approach leverages the Miss Cimory distribution program and aligns Cimory's commercial interest in selling dairy products with women's empowerment. Women like Elmita Sari Dewi are not just selling dairy products; they are building bridges to opportunity, empowerment, and a better tomorrow.

Enhancing women's financial independence. ADB's equity investment has helped Cimory expand its sales agent network from 2,509 agents in 2020 to 7,000 in 2024, empowering more women financially (photo by Robertus Pudyanto/ADB).

LESSONS AND KEY TAKEAWAYS

- Unusual but smart distribution models can open new markets, even for low-income groups or those in previously inaccessible locations. Utilizing a direct selling approach with a local distributors helps penetrate underserved markets in a cost-effective manner.
- Offering income opportunities to women with limited access to higher education or formal employment can create a sense of empowerment that not only creates dedicated and loyal sales agents, but also allows them to grow and to take on leadership roles in their communities. Encouraging local women to see themselves as entrepreneurs is a powerful tool. Businesses, families, and communities benefit from such transformational power.
- Miss Cimory distributors receive training that enhances their business skills, increasing their confidence and ability to succeed. Such training not only builds their sales skills but also strengthens their personal growth and community leadership.

Connecting with customers. Miss Cimory agents engage with customers one-on-one, ensuring that each delivery is personal and convenient (photo by Robertus Pudyanto/ADB).

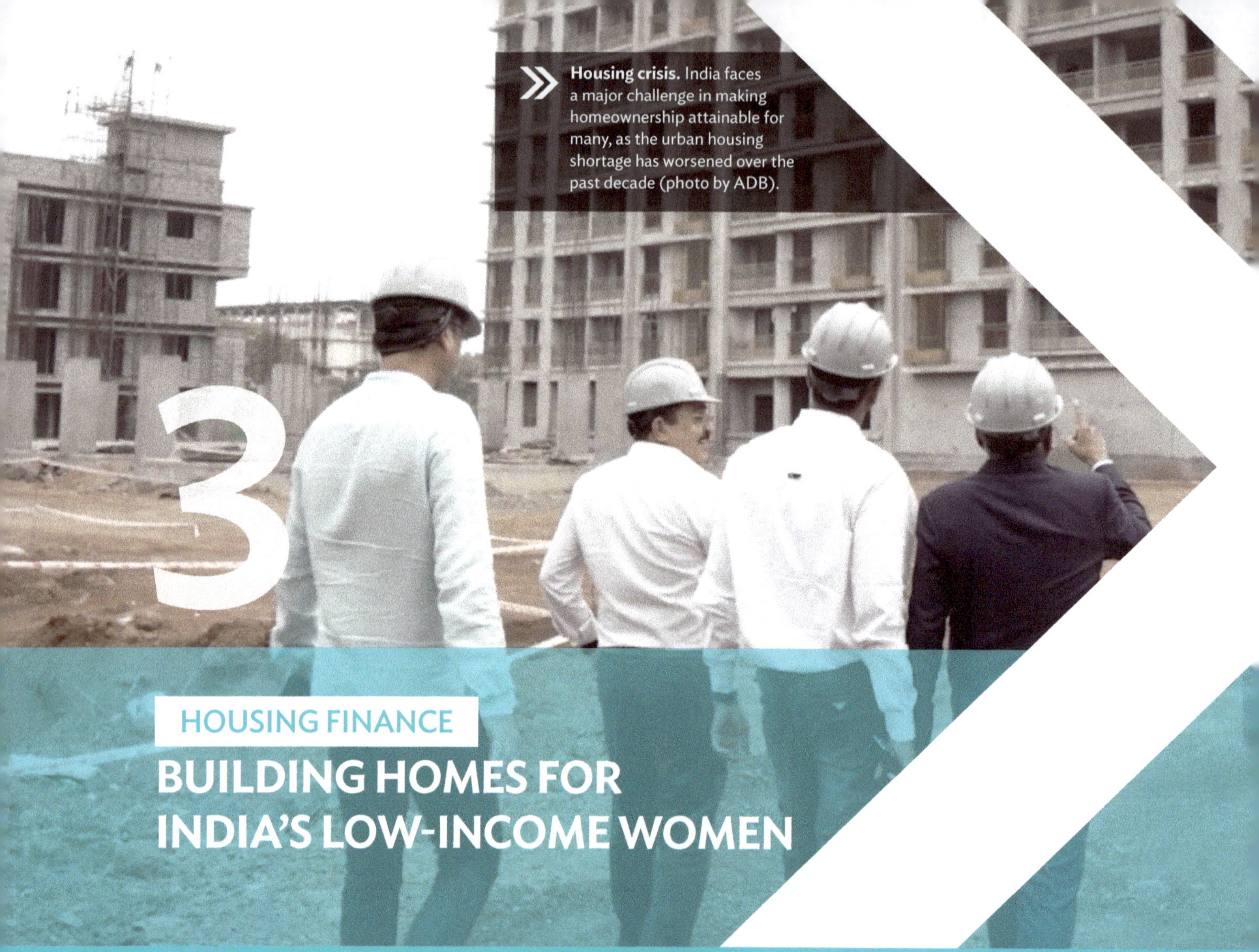

Housing crisis. India faces a major challenge in making homeownership attainable for many, as the urban housing shortage has worsened over the past decade (photo by ADB).

3

HOUSING FINANCE

BUILDING HOMES FOR INDIA'S LOW-INCOME WOMEN

PROJECT INFORMATION	
Project Name	IIFLHF Supporting Access to Affordable Green Housing for Women Project
Company	IIFL Home Finance Limited (IIFL HFL)
Country	India
ADB Loan	$58 million
Cofinancing	$10 million concessional loan from the Canadian Climate Fund for the Private Sector in Asia
Approval Date	3 December 2021
Development Goal	Improve availability of housing for low-income groups, particularly for women; and make building standards more climate friendly

Muskala Pushpa, a 40-year-old resident of rented housing in Kondapur, Hyderabad, and her family yearned for the stability and security that owning their own home would provide. Despite her husband's hard work as a security guard, homeownership felt out of reach for the family.

Pushpa had once before applied for a state government housing program. However, when her application was rejected, she was left with a deep sense of disappointment and insecurity. The uncertainty of renting weighed heavily on her, and she feared her dream of owning a home might never come true.

Everything changed when Pushpa learned about the housing initiative from IIFL Home Finance Limited (IIFL HFL).

IIFL HFL, a housing finance company providing affordable housing loans, secured a $68 million loan from ADB in 2022. This includes concessional cofinancing from the Canadian Climate Fund for the Private Sector in Asia, aimed at providing housing loans primarily to women borrowers or co-borrowers from low-income groups.

With a newfound sense of empowerment and determination, Pushpa fulfilled her dream by becoming the principal borrower of a housing loan worth ₹848,000 ($10,150) in 2022. The loan needs to be repaid over 15 years with a monthly payment of ₹8,601 ($103).

"Our family's goal has been to build or purchase our own house. It has finally turned into reality," Pushpa shared. The ease and speed with which IIFL HFL processed her loan application were a pleasant surprise, especially after her previous experiences with other housing loan programs. In addition to the quick processing time, the housing program offered competitive interest rates and flexible repayment options, making it even more beneficial for low-income families like hers.

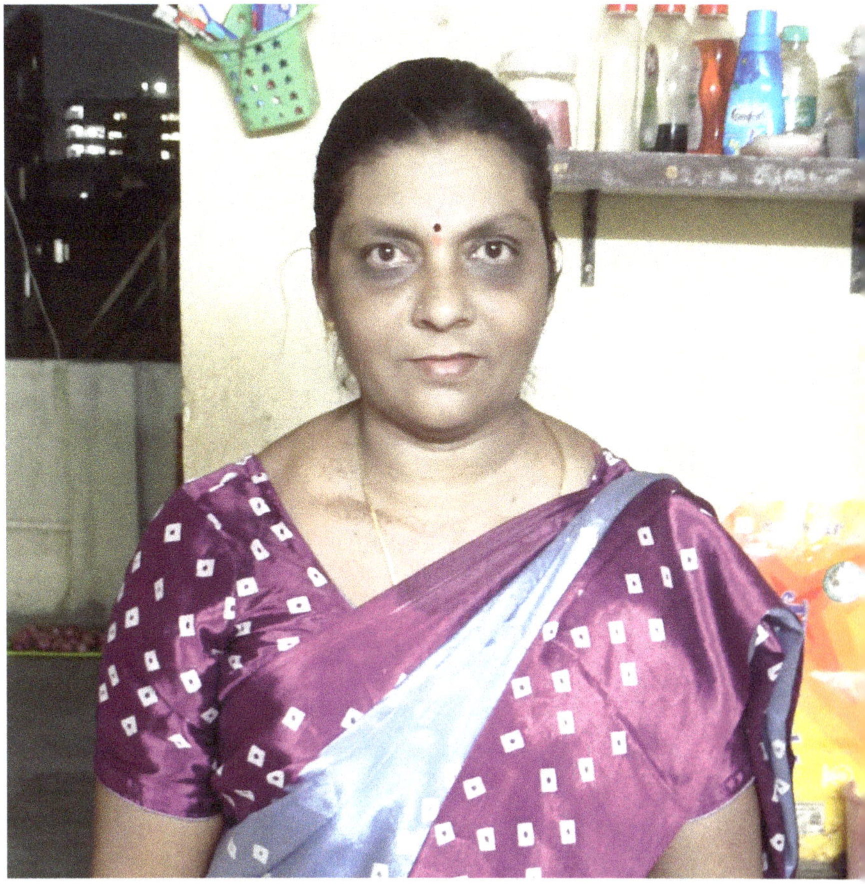

IIFL Home Finance Limited's affordable housing loans turned Muskala Pushpa's dream of homeownership into a reality (photo by IIFL HFL).

COMPANY PROFILE

IIFL Home Finance Limited

IIFL HFL provides affordable home loans to first-time home buyers from the economic weaker sections (EWS) and lower income groups (LIG) in India. With advanced IT infrastructure and an asset-light model, it ensures a seamless loan process, while expanding its reach across India with over 390 branches in 18 states. IIFL HFL is the leading corporate affordable housing finance company in India, with an average ticket size of ₹1,426,000 ($17,000).

Year Founded	2006
Head Office	Haryana, India
Primary Industry	Housing Finance
Number of Permanent Employees	5,436 (as of 30 September 2024)
Number of Active Customers	297,006 (as of 30 September 2024)
Website	www.iiflhomeloans.com

INDIA'S HOUSING FINANCE CHALLENGE

India faces a significant hurdle in making homeownership a reality for many. The country's urban housing shortage rose from 2012 to 2018 by 54% to 29 million units (Indian Council for Research on International Economic Relations 2020). More than 90% of this deficit was for the lower-income segment of the population (Jena 2016; Singh, Swaminathan, and Ramachandran 2013). However, most housing loans from finance companies go to middle- and high-income groups with incomes above ₹1 million ($12,034) (Rajan 2022).

India's mortgage penetration of just 11% of gross domestic product (Kousgi 2024) falls behind other nations. Limited access to housing finance arises from several key reasons. First, long-term funds are not widely available. Second, low-income households have additional challenges as they find themselves often excluded because they struggle to meet formal documentation requirements and income verification. Finally, there is a gender disparity in property ownership, as the tradition of male ownership limits women's access to housing finance and reinforces social inequality. Lack of property ownership contributes to the low social status of women, vulnerability to poverty, and low bargaining power within the household.

Beyond finance, India urgently needs to focus on improving building standards. According to India's Ministry of Environment, Forest and Climate Change (2021), the real estate and construction sectors account for 32% of India's greenhouse gas emissions, covering both operational and embodied carbon. Reducing these building-related emissions through sustainable, eco-friendly, and resilient construction is crucial to achieving the country's ambitious climate targets, like reducing emission intensity of gross domestic product by 45% by 2030, compared to 2005 (Press Information Bureau 2023).

In 2015, the government created the Pradhan Mantri Awas Yojana (PMAY), or the Housing for All program, to ensure that every eligible urban household has access to a pucca, a permanent house of durable materials with water connection, a toilet, reliable electricity, and other essential amenities (Ministry of Housing and Urban Affairs 2016a). The PMAY scheme particularly target low-income segments, which are categorized in India as EWS and LIG:

- **EWS.** Households with an annual income up to ₹300,000 ($3,900) and a house size of not more than 30 square meters.
- **LIG.** Households with an annual income ranging from ₹300,001 to ₹600,000 ($3,900 to $7,800) and a house size of not more than 60 square meters.

The PMAY scheme provides interest subsidies on housing loans for EWS and LIG to make homeownership more affordable for these income groups (Ministry of Housing and Urban Affairs 2016b).

INCLUSIVE BUSINESS STRATEGY

Despite government support, there are still challenges in making these loans accessible and such houses affordable. The ADB financing tackles housing affordability head-on by focusing on the EWS and LIG segments. IIFL HFL provides loans for these houses and focuses on the EWS, LIG, and middle-income groups in urban areas. IIFL HFL's activities are aligned with the government's PMAY program.

IIFL HFL offers a solution called *Jhatpat* (quick and hassle-free) to make homeownership more accessible and inclusive. The approach uses technology to provide approval decisions in just 30 minutes. Bank staff visit borrowers to check documents digitally; the process eliminates the need for multiple trips to the bank and reduces paperwork. The goal is to extend housing finance benefits to underserved and low-income groups in India by focusing on affordability, accessibility, empowerment, and community development.

Monu Ratra, executive director and chief executive officer of IIFL HFL, said that partnering with ADB enhances the company's capacity to address housing challenges.

"Our partnership with ADB is both on financial and nonfinancial fronts, as we stay committed to our goal of a million first-time homebuyers with a focus on sustainable homes as well.

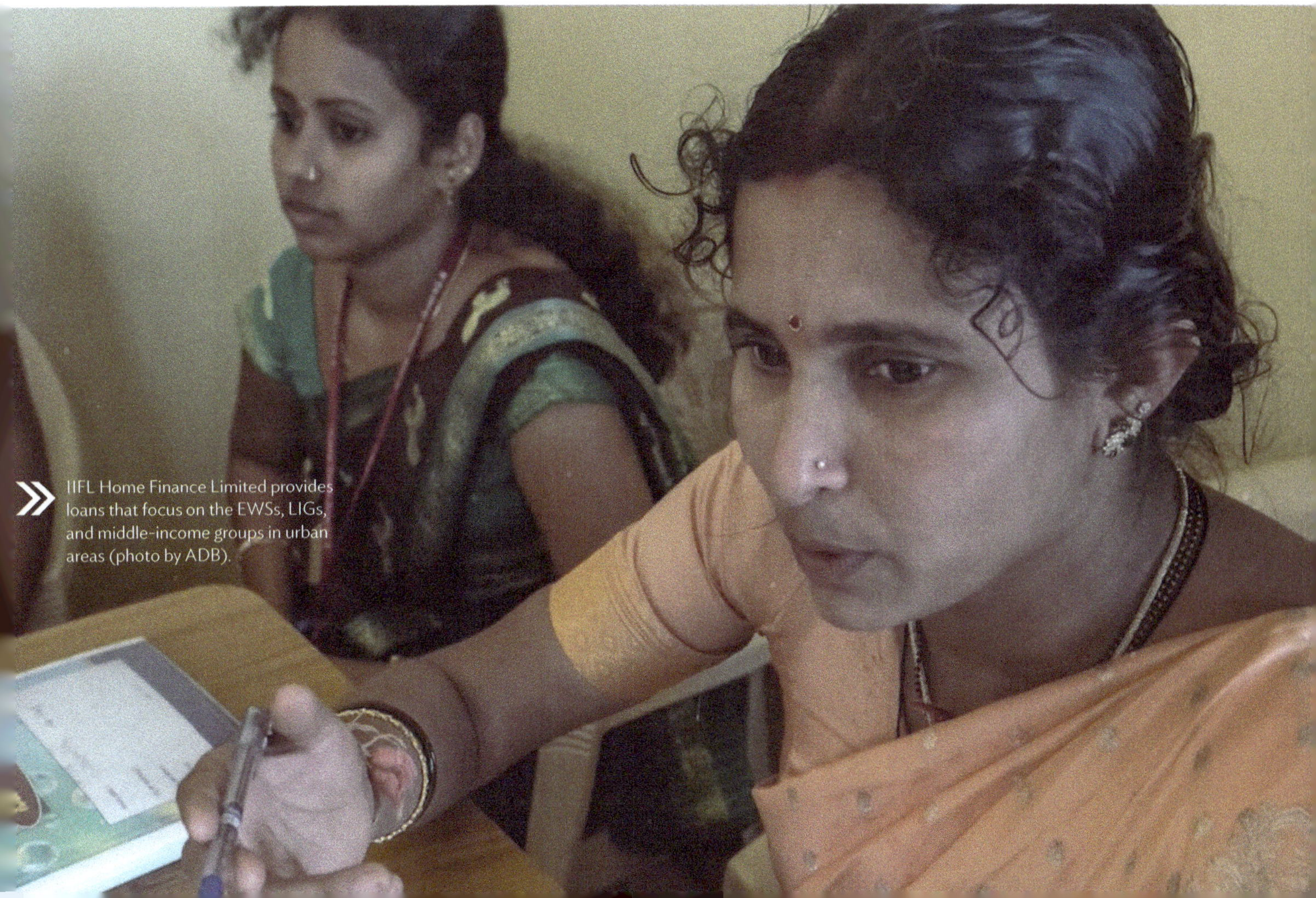

IIFL Home Finance Limited provides loans that focus on the EWSs, LIGs, and middle-income groups in urban areas (photo by ADB).

This partnership has really offered a unique blend of both to offer financial resources and expertise that complement IIFL HFL's business objectives. It facilitates the expansion of the company's lending portfolio for housing projects, green financing, and technical assistance, particularly in underserved areas," says Ratra. "ADB's involvement brings added value by increasing investor trust and encouraging stronger participation from lenders and stakeholders."

EMPOWERING WOMEN

Madhvi Gupta, head of marketing and corporate communications; environmental, social, and governance; and corporate social responsibility of IIFL HFL, said that the company's collaboration with ADB is envisioned "to create a profound and lasting impact on women's lives and their communities by fostering financial independence, promoting gender equality, and enhancing the quality of life."

One of the key strategies is to involve women as principal borrowers or co-signers in loan applications and mortgages. This approach not only provides women with financial independence but also strengthens their role in household decision-making and improves their social and economic standing in the community. As of February 2023, 95% of the total loans disbursed to EWS and LIG borrowers had women as borrowers or co-borrowers.

Committed to women's financial inclusion, IIFL HFL launched the SheCreates project, which was designed to empower women artisans by providing them with access to capital, mentorship, and training. ADB also helps IIFL HFL to enhance the development of women-friendly amenities in its project sites, and implement gender considerations such as adequate lighting, secure access points, and child-friendly spaces.

Empowering women. Through the SheCreates project, IIFL Home Finance Limited creates a supportive environment that fosters women's economic empowerment and contributes to their overall well-being (photo by IIFL HFL).

Pushpa now resides in a 45-square-meter home with her husband and their 10-year-old child. This new home is bigger and features a larger bedroom than their previous rented home. It is equipped with water-saving fixtures.

"I couldn't be happier with my current living situation," she said. "This is not just a house; it's a tangible embodiment of a dream we dared to chase, which now rests firmly within our grasp."

PROMOTING GREEN AFFORDABLE HOUSING

IIFL HFL's commitment to green housing practices is a cornerstone of its sustainability strategy. A major highlight is the recently launched *Humara Kutumb* (our family) project, which focuses on promoting affordable and sustainable housing solutions for homeowners. This flagship initiative helps everyday people access environmentally responsible housing options, advancing green building practices at the grassroots level.

IIFL HFL's Green Value Partners initiative focuses on promoting green affordable housing in India by assisting developers in every stage of their projects, ensuring compliance with local green building standards such as the Green Rating for Integrated Habitat Assessment and the Indian Green Building Council.

Our partnership with ADB is both on financial and nonfinancial fronts, as we stay committed to our goal of a million first-time homebuyers. ADB's involvement brings added value by increasing investor trust and encouraging stronger participation from lenders and stakeholders.

Monu Ratra
Executive Director and Chief Executive Officer
IIFL Home Finance Limited
India

Homes that comply with green building standards feature energy efficiency, and water conservation; and use eco-friendly, locally sourced, and recycled materials to reduce the carbon footprint and promote resource efficiency. The company integrates green housing principles into its housing loan products by "incentivizing sustainable housing choices."

Homebuyers who purchase properties in green buildings are eligible for reduced interest rates, which encourages the adoption of green building practices among developers and promotes environmentally friendly housing options for consumers.

This combined solution improves access to housing finance, and ultimately makes it easier for all households to find an affordable house.

Green homes, green future. IIFL Home Finance Ltd. integrates green housing principles into its housing loan products by "incentivizing sustainable housing choices" (photo by ADB).

Shared dream for women. Every Indian woman dreams to build a home for her family as a key step to securing a bright and stable future (photo by IIFL HFL).

LESSONS AND KEY TAKEAWAYS

- IIFL HFL's leveraging of a government program like the PMAY is an example of a partnership that potentiates the effect of these government programs and expands their outreach. PMAY reduces risks for IIFL HFL and makes the low-income segment commercially more attractive.
- Technology solutions like IIFL HFL's *Jhatpat* simplify the process, minimize paperwork, provides quick decisions, and can be tailored to address the specific challenges of low-income and underserved groups.
- Designing lending solutions that are affordable while ensuring profitability for the lending organization, combined with technical solutions tailored for low-income groups (like cost-efficient construction), can open up new markets and respond to previously suppressed demand.

Herding legacy. Birvaa Dashjamts has herded goats for 28 years, finding fulfillment in this generational tradition despite facing limited opportunities due to his limited education (photo by Bat-Erdene Batchuluun/ADB).

CASHMERE PRODUCTION

SCALING UP SUSTAINABLE CASHMERE IN MONGOLIA

PROJECT INFORMATION	
Project Name	Gobi Climate-Resilient Cashmere Value Chain Project
Company	Gobi Joint Stock Company
Country	Mongolia
ADB Financing	$30 million loan and up to $1 million technical assistance grant
Approval Date	26 October 2023
Financing Modality	Senior secured sustainability-linked loan facility
Development Goal	Support the climate resilience of cashmere herders in Mongolia.

Cashmere is renowned as one of the most luxurious and costly natural fibers. It is prized for its exceptional warmth, lightness, softness, and comfort. This fine wool is obtained by combing the undercoat of goats that inhabit cold, remote regions of Mongolia and the People's Republic of China.

Mongolia plays a crucial role in the global cashmere market, supplying an impressive 40% of the world's cashmere. From 2018 to 2022, the country produced about 10,000 to 12,000 tons of raw cashmere annually. However, a significant portion (85%–90%) of this raw cashmere is exported, with only a small fraction (10%–15%) being processed into finished products within the country (Mongolian Parliament 2020).

COMPANY PROFILE

Gobi Joint Stock Company

Gobi Joint Stock Company is a publicly listed company in Mongolia that produces luxury cashmere products. Its products are sold in three large retail stores in Ulaanbaatar, mainly to tourists, and internationally through their 35 overseas or online stores.

Year Founded	1981
Corporate Office	Ulaanbaatar, Mongolia
Primary Industry	Production and Sale of Cashmere Products
Total Number of Employees	1,765 (2023)
Revenue	MNT255.651 billion ($75 million)
Total Assets	MNT311.784 billion ($91 million)
Website	www.gobi.mn

Bayankhongor, a province heavily reliant on cashmere production, exemplifies Mongolia's dependence on herding as a way of life and livelihood. In the small Jinst *soum* (district), Birvaa Dashjamts has dedicated 28 years to herding goats, a tradition deeply rooted in his family and passed down through generations. Despite having limited education and few alternative opportunities, Birvaa finds fulfillment in this age-old practice.

Cashmere heritage. Founded in 1981, Gobi has become synonymous with high-quality cashmere textiles, sourcing raw materials from local herders in Mongolia (photo by ADB).

The region's extreme cold and harsh weather play a critical role in cashmere production. These conditions promote the growth of a dense, fine, and soft undercoat in cashmere goats, which are typically kept outdoors even during winter. This high-quality cashmere is a valuable resource, forming the backbone of the local economy.

However, these same weather conditions pose significant challenges. Severe winter events known as *dzuds*—characterized by prolonged cold, heavy snow, and temperatures as low as −30°C—endanger livestock survival

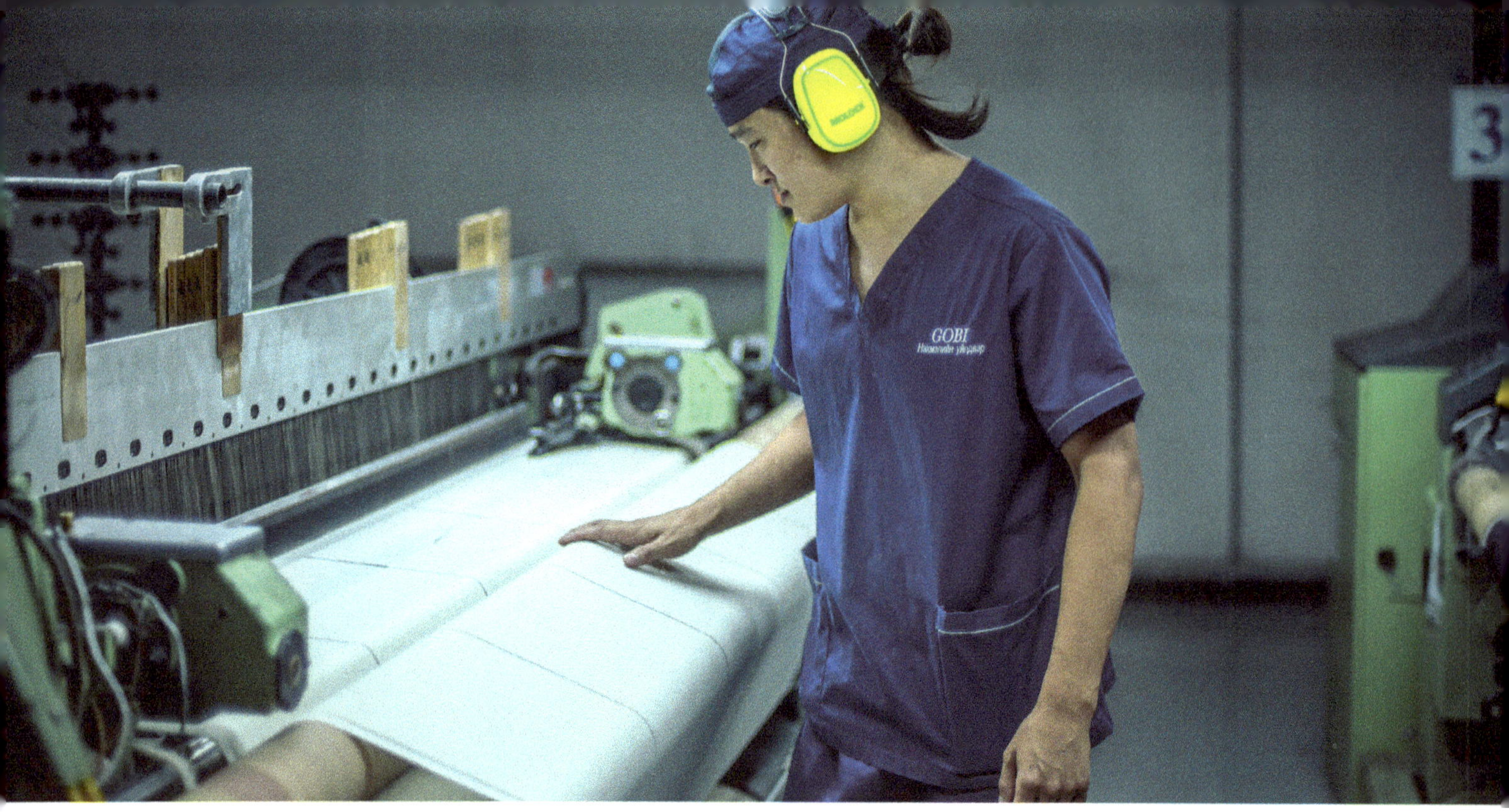

From pasture to product. Raw cashmere fibers collected from herders go through several detailed stages to become high-quality clothing (photo by Bat-Erdene Batchuluun/ADB)

and deplete herds. In recent years, these events have become more frequent and intense, exacerbated by the effects of climate change. Alongside *dzuds*, herders like Birvaa must now contend with additional climate threats, including heatwaves, droughts, and flooding. These challenges jeopardize the livelihoods of herders and threaten the sustainability of their way of life.

"The increasingly unpredictable weather patterns and extreme conditions have affected the health and productivity of our goat herds," said Birvaa. "On top of this, cashmere prices can also be volatile, which affects our income stability."

Mongolia has experienced 6 *dzuds* in the last 10 years, leading to significant livestock mortality (United Nations Office for the Coordination of Humanitarian Affairs 2024). After the 2022–2023 *dzud*, Mongolia lost 3 million or 11% of its total goat population (National Statistics Office of Mongolia 2024).

Herders collect high-quality cashmere from goats during spring when they naturally shed their soft undercoats. Using specialized combs, herders gently remove the undercoat fibers, which are then sorted to eliminate coarse hairs and impurities. This careful grooming and combing process ensures that the finest fibers are selected for processing. Despite being labor-intensive, a single goat yields only 115 to 380 grams of cashmere fiber per year, making the work both skilled and delicate.

Gobi Joint Stock Company is the largest cashmere manufacturer in Mongolia. To stand out in the global market, Gobi's goal is to leverage its rich heritage and superior quality and differentiate itself by emphasizing the authenticity, traceability, and sustainability of its products. But as it competes with the People's Republic of China's scale, efficiency, and advance technology, Gobi faces challenges with the reliability of supply from herders due to climate conditions, which directly affects their production.

To address these challenges, the company secured a loan of up to $30 million from ADB to expand its sustainable cashmere sourcing and production. An essential aspect of this expansion is to integrate more herders, such as Birvaa, directly into the cashmere value chain without the need for intermediary brokers. A grant-financed capacity development program aims to support nomadic herders in sustainable pasture management, enhance their understanding of basic pasture ecology, and provide training on financial literacy, budget management, and agro-economic models.

While the country's cashmere industry creates jobs for more than 300,000 herders who depend on their animals for survival, Bolormaa Batsuuri, Gobi's executive vice president for creative products, said that building a sustainable value chain is crucial because overgrazing from goats that are kept mainly for cashmere production can have environmental impacts leading to land degradation and desertification. "This sustainable value chain is imperative for us to ensure the future of cashmere and protect Mongolia's environment," said Bolormaa.

INCLUSIVE BUSINESS STRATEGY

Herders are integrated into the cashmere value chain through a systematic selection process based on criteria such as the quality of cashmere produced and the adoption of environmentally and socially sustainable and ethical animal husbandry practices.

"Herders meeting the criteria are included in the procurement process under fair pricing models. Our goal is to streamline the process by enabling herders to sell their cashmere directly at market rates, eliminating any unnecessary intermediaries that reduce their profits," Bolormaa said, emphasizing the support for the herders.

Blending tradition and innovation. Gobi combines traditional craftsmanship with modern technology, making it one of Mongolia's leading cashmere producers (photo by Bat-Erdene Batchuluun/ADB).

Gobi has implemented its Sustainable Cashmere Trilateral Project, which has received funding from ADB. The project emphasizes the importance of breeding, selecting, and sterilizing livestock, which is crucial for maintaining herd health and cashmere quality. Gobi believes that an improvement in the quality of raw materials sourced from individual animals will result in increased productivity and a reduction in overall animal numbers, thereby mitigating the adverse environmental impact of overgrazing.

The project provides high-quality male goats to ensure that their offspring meet optimal standards for cashmere production and quality. This approach results in superior cashmere yield per goat and, consequently, increased revenue per animal. Gobi's ultimate goal is to boost herders' income without increasing the overall number of goats.

Birvaa, with his 180 female goats, achieved a notable improvement in the quality of his raw cashmere after receiving 5 high-quality male goats from Gobi.

"Through this project, we advocate for animal health and the preservation of local breeds, which are well adapted to the harsh climate and environment, while educating young herders in the proper techniques for preparing goat cashmere. This will ultimately lead to an enhancement in both the yield and quality of raw materials," Bolormaa said. The project gives Gobi a range of benefits, including increasing resilience to climate change, stabilizing quality, and ensuring long-term supply.

ADB, Bolormaa added, was a perfect match for Gobi for this project because "the company's sustainable development policy of improving and increasing productivity and value within the framework of environment, society, and governance aligns with ADB's vision of a prosperous, inclusive, resilient, and sustainable Asia and the Pacific."

The herders from whom Gobi procures cashmere typically come from different socioeconomic profiles. Their average age varies, but many are middle-aged or older, ranging from their 30s to 60s.

Transforming lives. Through the ADB-financed project, Birvaa Dashjamts (right) and his family have experienced improved living conditions (photo by Bat-Erdene Batchuluun/ADB).

Empowered herders. Erdmaa Nyamdorj's participation in the ADB-supported Gobi project gave her and her husband new knowledge that is very relevant to their herding (photo by Bat-Erdene Batchuluun/ADB).

They primarily reside in rural areas of Mongolia, often in nomadic communities. This diversity underscores Gobi's inclusive business approach.

As a result of the project, an additional 106 herders have been integrated into the sustainable value chain of the cashmere industry.

TRAINING OPPORTUNITIES, STABILITY IN INCOME

Now that Gobi directly buys cashmere from him—with no intermediaries and with improved quality and volume of production—Birvaa said this gives him greater stability and predictability in his income. Before joining the project, his family earned MNT40 million ($11,765) annually. Their household income has increased to MNT45 million ($13,235) per year, thanks to Gobi's higher purchase prices—MNT147,000 ($43.24) per kilogram compared to the previous MNT110,000 ($32.35).

"Participating in the Gobi project has transformed our living conditions," said Birvaa. "The training and support have not only improved our income but also ensured the health and quality of our livestock. Most importantly, it has enabled us to secure a better future for our two children by affording them a good education."

Like Birvaa, 40-year-old Erdmaa Nyamdorj and her husband faced economic challenges while tending their herd for 14 years. Their greatest hope was to send their children to prestigious schools in Ulaanbaatar, a dream that seemed increasingly out of reach, especially after the devastating economic downturn of 2020, when cashmere prices plummeted because of the COVID-19 pandemic.

Before joining the project, Erdmaa's family earned a modest MNT32 million ($9,401) annually, barely enough to meet their basic needs. The low cashmere prices of 2020 hit them hard, leaving

Combing for quality. Birvaa Dashjamts carefully combs one of his goats to maintain its health and the quality of its coat (photo by Bat-Erdene Batchuluun/ADB).

them in a precarious financial situation. However, the implementation of the Gobi project transformed their lives. Through sustainable herding practices, improved animal health, and direct market access, their income in 2023 soared to MNT40 million ($11,752).

For Erdmaa, one helpful aspect of the project was the training on sterilization techniques. She learned the importance of sterilizing her male livestock during summer, which significantly improves the health, productivity, and climate resilience of her herd. The training also includes sessions on gender equality, equipping her with valuable knowledge and skills.

"One of the most significant changes in our family was moving from our traditional *ger*[4] into a spacious wooden house. The new home symbolized stability and comfort. Year after year, I am also able to improve my animal fencing, a proof of progress enabled by our participation in the Gobi project," she shared.

"The project equipped us with new information and knowledge that are very relevant to our herding, and to our lives as a whole," she added. "This holistic approach not only improved our herding practices but also enriched our lives, with a sense of empowerment and equality."

4 A portable, round tent used by nomadic people in Mongolia as a dwelling.

Nurturing her herd. Erdmaa Nyamdorj administers medication to one of her goats to ensure its overall health and well-being (photo by Bat-Erdene Batchuluun/ADB).

LESSONS AND KEY TAKEAWAYS

- Refining products that originate from traditional or culturally rooted raw materials and establishing value chains creates win-win situations where both the traditional or rural population and the national industry, and the country's image can benefit. Such value chains are ideal for inclusive business approaches.
- Providing training on key production practices can help producers, such as herders, improve the quality of their raw materials.
- Fair pricing models and long-term partnerships foster trust, loyalty, and sustainability within the producer community. Integrating producers based on specific criteria, such as quality and sustainability, strengthens their role within the value chain.

Improving access to quality health care. An ADB project is helping the Cygnus chain of hospitals in India to provide more affordable health-care services to low- and middle-income patients (photo by Amit Verma/ADB).

5

HEALTH CARE

BRIDGING THE HEALTH-CARE GAP IN UNDERSERVED INDIAN COMMUNITIES

PROJECT INFORMATION	
Project Name	Cygnus Affordable Hospitals Project
Company	Cygnus Medicare Private Limited
Country	India
ADB Financing	$18.4 million
Approval Date	28 August 2023
Financing Modality	Debt financing
Development Goal	Expand availability of high-quality, organized, and affordable health care in tier-2 and tier-3 cities in underserved regions of northern India

In the modest village of Fatehpur in Sonipat, Haryana lives Devi, an ordinary housewife dedicated to raising her three children while her husband manages a small shop. Fatehpur, like many other rural villages in India, often faces challenges in accessing quality health care because of its limitations in infrastructure and economic resources. The village has a population of 1,427 (Government of India n.d.).

COMPANY PROFILE

Cygnus Medicare Private Limited

Cygnus Medicare Private Limited (Cygnus) is an Indian health-care organization committed to delivering quality medical services and improving access to health care. It was established with a vision to transform the health-care sector by operating a network of hospitals and facilities that prioritize affordability and focus on underserved communities. Cygnus runs a chain of multispecialty hospitals under the brand name Ujala Cygnus. These hospitals are equipped with modern medical technology and staffed by qualified health-care professionals, offering a wide range of medical services, such as emergency care, surgical procedures, maternity care, and specialized treatments.

Year Established	2011
Head Office	New Delhi, India
Primary Industry	Health care
Number of Network Hospitals	22
Number of Doctors	300+
Number of Employees	1,198
Annual Revenue	₹4.39 billion ($52 million)
Website	www.ujalacygnus.com

In the first half of 2024, Devi's life took a tough turn when she fell severely ill while pregnant and approaching her due date. The local clinics in Fatehpur were not equipped to handle her condition. Even though they could choose to go to better hospitals further away, they were too far and too expensive to reach. The best option for her was Ujala Cygnus Hospital (UCH) Kaithal, a hospital run by Cygnus Medicare Private Limited, located 16 kilometers from her home.

INCLUSIVE HEALTH-CARE BUSINESS

Cygnus, established in 2011, has carved a niche in the health-care industry by focusing on underserved communities in India. Its unique approach involves operating hospitals in tier-2 cities (those with populations ranging from 0.5 to 5 million) and tier-3 cities (those with populations less than 0.5 million), where the need for medical care is often overlooked.

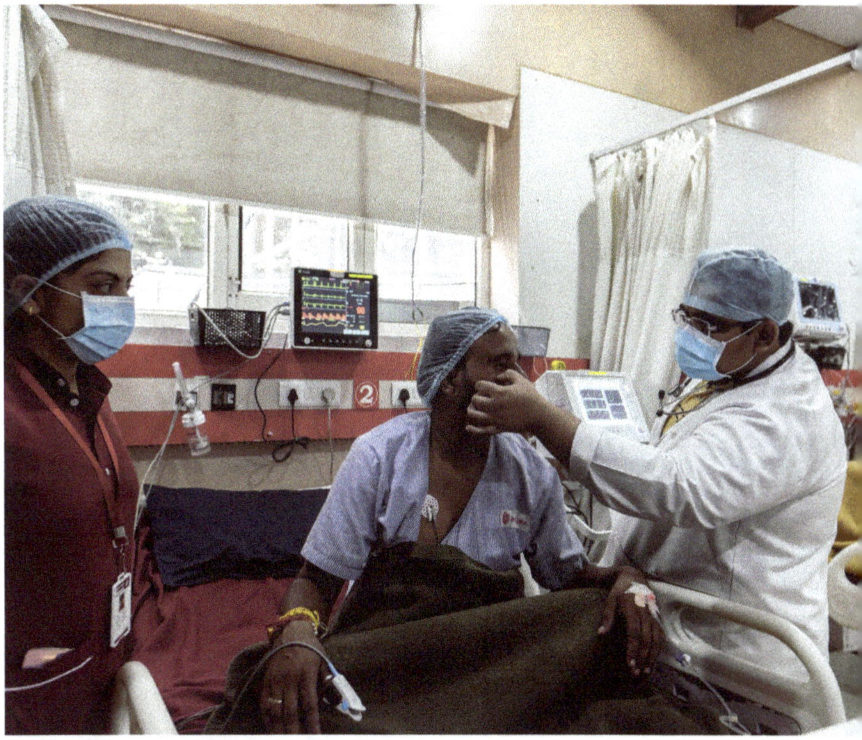

Affordable health care. Cygnus hospitals operate with low capital and operating costs, allowing them to charge 25%–30% less for services than other hospitals, making health care more affordable for low-income patients (photo by Amit Verma/ADB).

With 20 hospitals across 16 cities, Cygnus is committed to providing affordable health-care services to low- and middle-income patients. The company's model is particularly impactful in cities like Kaithal, classified as tier 3. Cygnus enhances access to quality hospitals and reduces health-care expenses, making its operation a consumer-driven inclusive business.

Cygnus, as an inclusive health-care company, adopts an asset-light model by renting poorly managed hospitals under a revenue-sharing deal rather than purchasing land and building new facilities. With low capital and operating costs, hospitals run by Cygnus can charge 25%–30% less for services compared to other hospitals, making them affordable to low-income patients.

Cygnus hospitals aim to provide affordable, accessible, and high-quality health-care services to underserved and low-income populations. Cygnus offers a range of subspecialty services such as cardiology, surgery, neurology, nephrology, orthopedics, gynecology, oncology, and dentistry, with more than 300 doctors and medical experts across its facilities (Ujala Cygnus n.d.). Cygnus also optimizes existing capacity and expands it to satisfy local demand for quality and affordable health care. Patients can access its services through direct visits, online appointments, satellite clinics, community health centers, health camps, and telemedicine.

Prateek Ghosal, chief of strategy, growth, and digital services of Cygnus, highlighted the shortage of specialized hospitals in smaller towns and rural areas.

Cygnus-run hospital in Kaithal, India. With funding from ADB, UCH Kaithal's bed capacity is expected to increase from 100 to 150 by 2026 (photo by Amit Verma/ ADB). .

Expanding health care. Patients wait outside the x-ray room at the UCH Kaithal. More low-income patients in India can now access quality health-care services as Cygnus expands and builds more specialty facilities (photo by Amit Verma/ADB).

"Most high-quality hospitals are concentrated in major cities or metropolitan areas. Consequently, the accessibility of hospitals for the general public and poor people is not very good. Residents of smaller towns often have to rely on government hospitals, which typically do not have specialty or super-specialty doctors available," said Ghosal.

In 2023, ADB signed a loan agreement for ₹1.5 billion ($18.4 million) with Cygnus. This financing enables Cygnus to lease six hospitals and improve existing ones by adding subspecialty departments and increasing bed capacity from 1,622 to 2,560 by 2026.

The new hospitals will also serve patients covered by India's national health insurance program—Ayushman Bharat-Pradhan Mantri Jan Arogya Yojana (AB-PMJAY)—facilitating easier access to health care for individuals in need. AB-PMJAY aims to provide free health insurance coverage to low-income earners in the country.

The financing from ADB has significantly bolstered our capabilities in terms of increased capacity, hospital expansion, and the building of more specialty facilities. We are now able to provide treatment to more low-income patients, ensuring that more economically disadvantaged individuals have access to quality health-care services.

Prateek Ghosal
Chief of Strategy, Growth and Digital
Cygnus Medicare Private Limited
India

"The financing from ADB has significantly bolstered our capabilities in terms of increased capacity, hospital expansion, and the building of more specialty facilities. We are now able to provide treatment to more low-income patients, ensuring that more economically disadvantaged individuals have access to quality health-care services," said Ghosal.

"With the support from ADB, we have been able to upgrade our clinical facilities significantly. This includes the acquisition of advanced medical equipment, the implementation of cutting-edge health-care technologies, and the enhancement of our overall infrastructure to ensure the highest standards of patient care."

SCALING UP SERVICES AND BED CAPACITY

When patient Devi was admitted to UCH Kaithal hospital, she was provided with the necessary consultations, diagnostic tests, and medical procedures. She stayed at the hospital for 4 days and received comprehensive care from skilled doctors and cooperative staff.

"I didn't have access to any other nearby hospitals," Devi recalled. "I chose this hospital because of its good reputation for providing quality treatment and having highly regarded doctors, on top of being the most accessible facility from where I live."

Devi praised the hospital's cleanliness, the expertise of the medical staff, and the overall care she received. She delivered her baby girl and received a gynecological procedure afterward, something she could not have easily undergone in other hospitals.

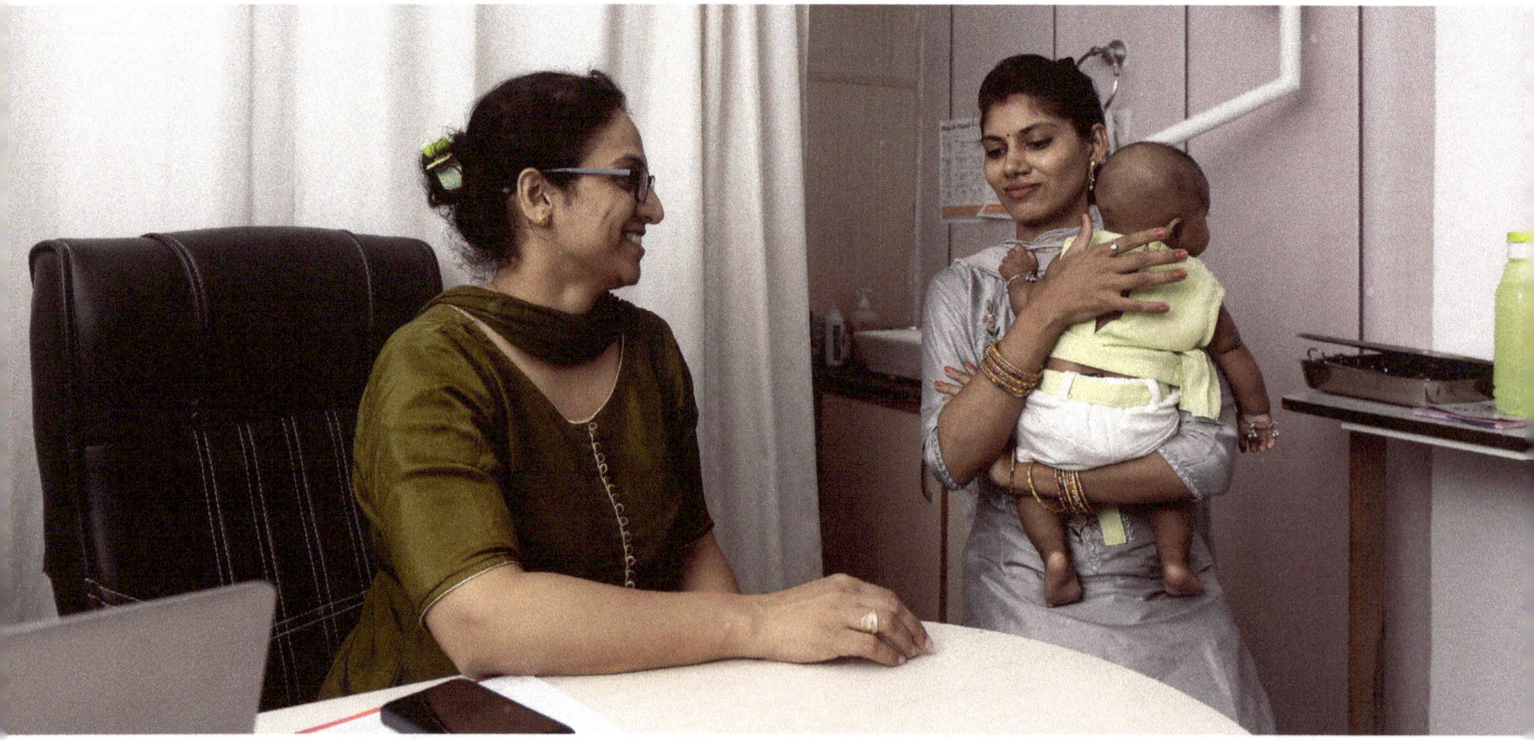

Mother and child care. Devi visits her doctor for a routine checkup with her baby. Cygnus hospitals in India offer a range of support for pregnant mothers, including pre-delivery consultations, safe delivery facilities, and essential postnatal care with skilled medical staff on hand for regular and complex deliveries (photo by Amit Verma/ADB).

Her financial burden was alleviated, thanks to the hospital's partnership with AB-PMJAY. She did not need to pay anything upon discharge.

"My experience at this hospital was excellent," Devi shared. "The staff were very cooperative and well educated, the doctors were highly skilled, and the overall cleanliness and care were commendable. It would really be such great news to our community if their bed capacity and services get expanded."

UCH Kaithal can accommodate a total of 100 patients at any given time. Through the ADB financing, it is expected to increase its bed capacity to 150 by 2026.

The ideal hospital bed to population ratio in India is 3 beds per 1,000 people, as recommended by the World Health Organization. However, India's current ratio is 1.3 beds per 1,000 people (Press Trust of India 2023). This means India has a significant gap to bridge to meet international health-care standards.

Health care for all. A patient checks in at the registration desk inside the UCH Kaithal (photo by Amit Verma/ADB).

IMPACT BEYOND HEALTH

In a country where health-care disparity remains a pressing issue, the efforts of organizations like Cygnus toward an inclusive health-care business are crucial. In addressing the health and medical needs of underserved residents in tier-2 and tier-3 cities, Cygnus is not only bridging the health-care gap and improving individual health outcomes, but also enhancing the overall quality of life in these communities. The presence of such hospitals reduces the need for long-distance travel to metropolitan areas for medical care, thereby reducing financial strain and emotional stress for patients and their families.

Affordable care close to home. Cygnus patients benefit from cost savings on consultations, treatments, and access to specialized services in their local areas (photo by Amit Verma/ADB).

LESSONS AND KEY TAKEAWAYS

- Focusing on tier-2 and tier-3 cities, where medical care is often lacking, is a key aspect of Cygnus's inclusive business strategy. Targeting underserved regions allows businesses to address unmet demand while creating social impact. Providing accessible and affordable health care to these populations also helps build a loyal customer base.
- Cygnus's innovative asset-light model—renting distressed or operationally mismanaged hospitals rather than investing in new infrastructure—reduces capital expenditure, enabling quicker market entry and flexibility. This business model can be replicated in other industries seeking to scale rapidly while keeping operating costs low.
- Offering a wide range of subspecialty services (e.g., cardiology, surgery, oncology) across various locations enables Cygnus to meet the diverse medical needs of underserved communities. Expanding service offerings is critical for creating a one-stop solution for consumers, reducing the need for them to seek out specialists in faraway metropolitan areas, which can be both costly and time-consuming.
- By aligning with government initiatives such as AB-PMJAY, Cygnus ensures that low-income patients can access health-care services at no or minimal cost. Tapping into national insurance programs not only ensures a stable revenue stream but also boosts access to care for marginalized groups. Businesses can explore partnerships with government schemes to increase the affordability and reach of their services.
- Cygnus offers patients multiple ways to access health care, including direct visits, online appointments, telemedicine, health camps, and satellite clinics. Creating varied channels for service delivery ensures broader access, particularly for patients in remote areas, and increases convenience for all consumers. Diversification of access points can be critical in scaling an inclusive business model.

Patients wait in the lobby of UCH Kaithal hospital (photo by Amit Verma/ADB).

REFERENCES

Asia Pacific Foundation of Canada. 2018. *2018 Survey of Entrepreneurs and MSMEs in the Philippines: Building the Capacity of MSMEs Through Market Access.* https://apfcanada-msme.ca/wp-content/uploads/2024/04/2018-Survey-of-Entrepreneurs-and-MSMEs-in-the-Philippines_0.pdf.

Asian Development Bank. 2018. *Inclusive Business Financing: Where Commercial Opportunity and Sustainability Converge.* https://www.adb.org/sites/default/files/publication/433706/inclusive-business-financing.pdf.

Desai, J. 2024. Deal Focus: General Atlantic Buys India Hospital Chain to Tap Affordable Healthcare Push. Ion Analytics. *Mergermarket.* 30 April. https://ionanalytics.com/insights/mergermarket/deal-focus-general-atlantic-buys-india-hospital-chain-to-tap-affordable-healthcare-push/.

Food and Agriculture Organization of the United Nations. 2019. *Country Gender Assessment of Agriculture and the Rural Sector in Indonesia.* https://openknowledge.fao.org/server/api/core/bitstreams/2b3ec098-9fb2-45e4-a010-47442291ba30/content.

Government of India. n.d. *Fatehpur Population – Sonipat, Haryana – Census 2011.* https://www.census2011.co.in/data/village/59844-fatehpur-haryana.html.

Hammond, A. et al. 2007. *The Next 4 Billion: Market Size and Business Strategy at the Base of the Pyramid.* International Finance Corporation and World Resources Institute. https://wriorg.s3.amazonaws.com/s3fs-public/pdf/n4b_fulltext_hi.pdf.

Indian Council for Research on International Economic Relations. 2020. *Urban Housing Shortage in India: 2018 Update.*

International Business Action Network. 2021. *Inclusive Business Features: The Distinguishing Characteristics of Businesses that Engage the Base of the Pyramid.* https://www.inclusivebusiness.net/sites/default/files/2022-03/Inclusive%2BBusiness%2BFeatures %28002%29.pdf.

Jena, M. 2016. UN Expert Calls for India to Ramp up Action to Help Slum Dwellers. *Reuters.* 25 April. https://www.reuters.com/article/world/u-n-expert-calls-for-india-to-ramp-up-action-to-help-slum-dwellers-idUSKCN0XM1X7/.

Khor, N., I. Sebastian, and R. Aldaba. 2013. Enterprises in the Philippines: Dynamism and Constraints to Employment Growth. ADB Economics Working Paper Series. No. 334. https://www.adb.org/sites/default/files/publication/59604/ewp-334.pdf.

Kousgi, G. 2024. Navigating the Mortgage Landscape: Vision for Affordable Housing Finance. *The Hindu Business Line.* 11 March. https://www.thehindubusinessline.com/money-and-banking/navigating-the-mortgage-landscape-vision-for-affordable-housing-finance/article67938628.ece (accessed 14 June 2024).

Kusumadewi, A. R. and H. Soedjito. 2018. The role of women farmers in rural development: A case study in Indonesia. *Pertanika Journal of Social Sciences & Humanities.* 26 (2). pp. 821–832.

Ministry of Environment, Forest and Climate Change, Government of India. 2021. *India: Third Biennial Update Report to the United Nations Framework Convention on Climate Change.* https://unfccc.int/sites/default/files/resource/INDIA_%20BUR-3_20.02.2021_High.pdf.

Ministry of Housing and Urban Affairs, Government of India. 2016a. Pradhan Mantri Awas Yojana: Housing for All (Urban) Scheme Guidelines. March 2016. https://mohua.gov.in/upload/uploadfiles/files/18HFA_guidelines_March2016-English.pdf.

Ministry of Housing and Urban Affairs, Government of India. 2016b. Press Note on Economically Weaker Section (EWS) and Low-Income Group (LIG) Beneficiary Categories. Press Information Bureau. https://pib.gov.in/PressNoteDetails.aspx?NoteId=151895&ModuleId=3&reg=3&lang=1.

Mongolian Parliament. 2020. Resolution on the Approval of the Action Plan of the Government of Mongolia for 2020–2024. Ulaanbaatar.

National Statistics Office of Mongolia. 2024. *Number of Goats in Mongolia for the Year 2022 and 2023.* https://www.1212.mn/en (accessed 20 November 2024).

Philippine Department of Trade and Industry. n.d. *Philippine MSME Statistics.* https://www.dti.gov.ph/resources/msme-statistics/ (accessed 15 July 2024).

Press Information Bureau; Government of India. 2023. India achieves two targets of Nationally Determined Contribution well ahead of the time. https://pib.gov.in/PressReleaseIframePage.aspx?PRID=1987752.

Press Trust of India. 2023. India Needs Additional 2.4 Million Hospital Beds to Reach Recommended Ratio: Report. *The Economic Times*. https://economictimes.indiatimes.com/news/india/india-needs-additional-2-4-million-hospital-beds-to-reach-recommended-ratio-report/articleshow/105450555.cms?from=mdr.

Rajan, J. 2022. Gender-Inclusive Fiscal Incentives for Green Affordable Housing in India. *IIFL Home Finance Limited (IIFL HFL).* https://www.iiflhomeloans.com/blogs/gender-inclusive-fiscal-incentives-green-affordable-housing-india.

Singh, S., M. Swaminathan, and V. K. Ramachandran. 2013. Housing Shortages in Rural India. *Review of Agrarian Studies.* 3 (2). pp. 54–72.

UBS. 2023. *Global Wealth Report 2024.* https://www.ubs.com/content/dam/assets/wm/static/noindex/wm-germany/2024/doodownload/Global-Wealth-Report-2024.pdf.

Ujala Cygnus. https://ujalacygnus.com.

United Nations Children's Fund (UNICEF). 2020. *The Impact of the COVID-19 Crisis on Households in the National Capital Region of the Philippines.* https://www.unicef.org/philippines/media/2581/file/TheImpactofCOVID-19CrisisonHouseholdsinNCR.pdf.

United Nations Development Programme (UNDP). 2020. MSME Value Chain Rapid Response Survey. https://www.undp.org/philippines/publications/msme-value-chain-rapid-response-survey (accessed 20 November 2024).

United Nations Office for the Coordination of Humanitarian Affairs. 2024. Mongolia: Dzud Response Plan (Dec 2023–June 2024). https://www.unocha.org/publications/report/mongolia/mongolia-dzud-response-plan-dec-2023-june-2024-issued-25-march-2024.

World Bank. 2024. Poverty and Inequality Platform (version 20240627_2017_01_02_PROD). World Bank Group. www.pip.worldbank.org. (accessed 19 October 2024).

Journey to safe motherhood. Devi and her child benefited from Cygnus hospitals' commitment to providing accessible, quality maternity care to low-income families in India (photo by Amit Verma/ADB).

www.ingramcontent.com/pod-product-compliance
Lightning Source LLC
Chambersburg PA
CBHW041758220926
51847CB00014B/249
9789292770778